GREAT CAREERS IN
NATURE

by Connor Stratton

FOCUS
READERS.

NAVIGATOR

WWW.FOCUSREADERS.COM

Focus Readers is distributed by North Star Editions:
sales@northstareditions.com | 888-417-0195

Produced for Focus Readers by Red Line Editorial.

Photographs ©: Shutterstock Images, cover, 1, 8–9, 13, 14–15, 17, 19, 21, 22–23, 25, 26–27; iStockphoto, 4–5, 11; Red Line Editorial, 29

Library of Congress Cataloging-in-Publication Data
Names: Stratton, Connor, author.
Title: Great careers in nature / Connor Stratton.
Description: Lake Elmo, MN : Focus Readers, [2022] | Series: Great careers| Includes index. | Audience: Grades 4-6
Identifiers: LCCN 2021011874 (print) | LCCN 2021011875 (ebook) | ISBN 9781644938461 (hardcover) | ISBN 9781644938928 (paperback) | ISBN 9781644939383 (ebook) | ISBN 9781644939802 (pdf)
Subjects: LCSH: Natural history--Vocational guidance--Juvenile literature.
Classification: LCC QH49 .S77 2022 (print) | LCC QH49 (ebook) | DDC 508.023--dc23
LC record available at https://lccn.loc.gov/2021011874
LC ebook record available at https://lccn.loc.gov/2021011875

Printed in the United States of America
Mankato, MN
082021

ABOUT THE AUTHOR

Connor Stratton writes and edits nonfiction children's books. He loves going on hikes and exploring the natural world.

TABLE OF CONTENTS

CHAPTER 1

NATURE IS EVERYWHERE

When people think about careers in nature, they might imagine park rangers or forestry workers. However, these are only two of the many careers that involve working in nature.

Nature is everywhere. And people are always learning more about it. In fact, careers in nature often involve science.

One of a park ranger's jobs is to help visitors gain a better understanding of the park.

For example, many people work in Earth sciences. These fields study the planet's many parts and the systems they form. Some scientists study how rocks change over time. Others study water systems on Earth. And some scientists study the weather and climate.

Many nature careers focus on living things. One growing field is **environmental** science. This field focuses on humans. It often looks at how people impact the world. Some scientists study the negative impacts of **climate change**. Others work to solve those problems.

Conservation is another important field. Conservation workers manage natural lands and parks. They make sure these areas remain healthy. That way, everyone can enjoy them. Protecting Earth's wonders is a key part of all careers in nature. And working outdoors is a great bonus.

WORKING IN NATURE

There are many great careers that involve working in nature. This table shows just a few.

EARTH SCIENCES	ENVIRONMENTAL SCIENCES	CONSERVATION
Seismologists	Biologists	Conservation Scientists
Geologists	Ecologists	Foresters
Oceanographers	Environmental Scientists	Park Rangers
Hydrologists	Technicians	Wildland Firefighters
Meteorologists	Environmental Engineers	
Climatologists		

CHAPTER 2

EARTH SCIENCES

There are three main kinds of Earth sciences. One kind focuses on Earth's solid, physical features. For example, geologists study how the planet has changed over time. To do so, they often look at rocks and minerals. Some geologists visit specific areas. They take rock **samples** and study them.

A geologist may take many different rock samples from an area.

A second type of Earth science focuses on water. Some scientists are oceanographers. They might study ocean tides, waves, or currents. They might also research the ocean floor.

Hydrologists study parts of the water cycle. They look at rain and snow. They study groundwater. They also study rivers, lakes, and oceans. Often, hydrologists look at water quality. They might take samples from a river. They test the samples for pollution.

The third kind of Earth science looks at the atmosphere. Meteorologists focus on weather. Some develop weather forecasts. They often use computer models. They

Hydrologists may take kits into nature so they can study the water quality of a stream.

try to predict what future weather will be.

Other meteorologists report the weather.

Many work for TV stations. Extreme

weather can be a big part of the job.

Some meteorologists study it up close.

They might follow tornadoes. Others travel to huge storms for reporting. They explain what the conditions are like.

Many atmospheric scientists study Earth's climate. They are called climatologists. These scientists look at weather patterns over long periods of

THE NATURE BEAT

Some people who work in nature are reporters. Reporters may travel to extreme weather events, such as hurricanes. Others go to places in the wild. They might report on at-risk animals. Some reporters focus on climate change. They travel to areas affected by the crisis. They explain what it's like to live there.

Some climatologists study tree rings to find out how an area's climate has changed over the years.

time. Some climatologists focus on the past. They study what Earth's climate was like long ago. Others focus on the present. They look at how Earth's climate is changing right now. They study the human-caused climate crisis.

CHAPTER 3

LIFE AND ENVIRONMENTAL SCIENCES

Many careers in nature involve biology. This field is the study of life. Some biologists study animals in the wild. They often focus on a particular type of animal. Other biologists study plants. And some focus on tiny organisms. Ecology is a related field. Ecologists study how living things relate to their environments.

Biologists may return to the same area many times to observe changes in plant life.

These scientists look at how **species** adapt. For example, they might study how plants survive in the desert.

Environmental science is similar to ecology. But it focuses on humans. Some scientists study how the climate crisis will affect **ecosystems**. Others focus on health and safety. They look at how the environment impacts people. Scientists might look at air pollution. They study how that pollution harms people.

People have damaged many areas already. For instance, some places are filled with toxic waste. Governments try to clean these places. They often depend on environmental scientists.

Some environmental scientists study polluted areas and work on ways to clean them.

The scientists visit the sites. They plan how to clean up each site. Then they oversee the cleaning process.

Some environmental scientists study future projects. They look at how risky a project could be. For example, a company might try to build a new oil pipeline. Scientists study the pipeline's impact. They might figure out how harmful a pipeline leak would be. Then they report their findings. That knowledge helps decide whether projects go forward.

Technicians help environmental scientists. They help carry out research

ENGINEERING NATURE

Environmental engineers work to solve environmental problems. Many engineers design systems to clean wastewater. Others address pollution. Some even study climate engineering. This field tries to reverse climate change. Workers might develop technologies to take greenhouse gases out of the air. Or they might find ways to cool the planet. These changes can bring their own risks. But engineers try to think creatively to solve tough problems.

Technicians may help environmental scientists gather samples of polluted soil.

and gather data. For example, technicians might help keep track of pollution levels in a certain area. They collect samples of soil or water. They test those samples in a lab. Then technicians prepare reports on their findings.

SCUBA DIVING FOR SCIENCE

Most of the ocean is unexplored by humans. It is home to many mysteries. Marine biologists explore these mysteries up close. They might focus on one species. For example, some scientists study orcas. They often take boats out on the ocean. They find and track orcas. They study the animals' behaviors.

Other marine biologists study ecosystems. Many look at coral reefs. These living systems are home to a huge variety of species. Biologists study species' relationships to one another. They might scuba dive to a reef. They swim among the corals. They pay attention to what they see.

Some scientists are deep-sea biologists. They might take submarines to the seafloor. These

Some marine biologists dive underwater to observe animals in their natural habitat.

scientists study previously unseen parts of the ocean. Sometimes they discover new species. It is an exciting field for people who love the unknown.

CHAPTER 4

CONSERVATION

Conservation workers help manage natural resources and lands. Some workers are scientists. They plan how people can use natural resources and lands. They also help protect parks and **preserves**.

Foresters oversee the planting of new trees. They restore forests. They work

Foresters help make sure people use forests responsibly.

to prevent wildfires, too. Foresters also manage the chopping down of trees. They respond to demands for lumber. But they work to limit environmental harm.

WILDLAND FIREFIGHTERS

Fighting wildfires is much different than putting out building fires. Some wildland firefighters try to stop fires early. They take helicopters to the source. They use ropes to drop to the ground. Then they try to put the fire out. Other teams are called hotshots. They focus on the worst part of a fire. The work is very dangerous. But these workers save many people, animals, and natural areas. Climate change is causing more wildfires. So, wildland firefighters are more important than ever.

Wildland firefighters often use helicopters and planes to help put out blazes.

Other workers help foresters and conservation scientists. They often perform the day-to-day tasks. These workers plant new trees. They also spray chemicals to remove harmful insects.

Park rangers work in state and national parks. Some help with research. Others lead students on field trips. They teach young people about the parks' features.

CHAPTER 5

ENTERING THE FIELD

Some careers in nature can begin after high school. For example, forest and conservation workers are trained on the job. Many workers learn to clear certain trees. Then the rest of the forest has more space to grow.

Other careers require two-year associate's degrees. Environmental

Taking science classes can be a great way to prepare for a career in nature.

technicians are one example. But many careers require four-year college degrees. People often study environmental science. They also take courses in Earth and life sciences. Jobs involving research typically require advanced degrees.

People take entry-level jobs after finishing school. They work with people who have more experience. They learn specific skills on the job. Some learn to use advanced equipment. Others learn how to handle toxic waste. With more experience, people can move up in their careers.

Some skills are helpful in many different nature careers. For example, working in nature can be physically tough. It requires **stamina**. Problem-solving skills are also helpful. Thinking critically is, too. Most of all, people must love nature. It is incredibly rewarding to help protect the planet.

CAREER PREP CHECKLIST

Interested in a career in nature? As you move into middle school and high school, try these steps.

1 Study hard in school. Take as many science classes as you can.

2 Tell a guidance counselor about your interest. This person can help you find opportunities to get experience in nature.

3 Be a citizen scientist. Test the water quality at a nearby body of water. Collect weather data. Ask a teacher or librarian how to get involved.

4 Visit nearby state and national parks or preserves. Ask employees for tours. And ask them about their experiences working there.

5 Find the national parks that have junior ranger programs. These can be great opportunities to see what it would be like to work as a ranger.

6 See if your area has summer camps or after-school programs in nature. Use the internet to find these opportunities.

FOCUS ON
GREAT CAREERS
IN NATURE

Write your answers on a separate piece of paper.

1. Write a paragraph explaining the main ideas of Chapter 3.

2. Do you think Earth science or environmental science is more interesting? Why?

3. Which of these jobs is an example of a conservation career?

> **A.** meteorologist
> **B.** forester
> **C.** deep-sea biologist

4. How is environmental science similar to ecology?

> **A.** Both focus on how the climate crisis affects an area's weather.
> **B.** Both focus on how living things relate to their environments.
> **C.** Both focus on the ways humans are changing the planet.

Answer key on page 32.

GLOSSARY

climate change
A human-caused global crisis involving long-term changes in Earth's temperature and weather patterns.

conservation
The careful protection of plants, animals, and natural resources so they are not lost or wasted.

ecosystems
Communities of living things and how they interact with their surrounding environments.

environmental
Related to the natural surroundings of living things in a particular place.

preserves
Areas of land set aside for managing and protecting animals and plants.

samples
Small pieces taken from a larger object or living thing for study.

species
Groups of animals or plants that are alike and can breed with one another.

stamina
The ability to continue working for a long time.

TO LEARN MORE

BOOKS

Bedell, J. M. *So, You Want to Work with Animals? Discover Fantastic Ways to Work with Animals, from Veterinary Science to Aquatic Biology.* New York: Aladdin, 2017.

Braun, Eric. *Brink of Extinction: Can We Stop Nature's Decline?* North Mankato: Capstone Press, 2021.

Huddleston, Emma. *Studying Climate Change.* Minneapolis: Abdo Publishing, 2021.

NOTE TO EDUCATORS

Visit **www.focusreaders.com** to find lesson plans, activities, links, and other resources related to this title.

INDEX